MY FIRST SCIENCE B·O·O·K

ANGELA WILKES

DORLING KINDERSLEY · LONDON

Art Editor Thomas Keenes
Photography Dave King

Managing Art Editor Roger Priddy

[DK]

A Dorling Kindersley Book

First published in Great Britain in 1990 by
Dorling Kindersley Publishers Limited,
9 Henrietta Street, London WC2E 8PS

Reprinted 1990, 1991

British Library Cataloguing in Publication Data

Wilkes, Angela
  My first science book.
  1. Science
  I. Title
  500
  ISBN 0−86318−451−0

Phototypeset by Bookworm Typesetting
Colour reproduction by Colorscan, Singapore
Printed in Italy by LEGO

Dorling Kindersley would like to thank Penny Britchfield,
Jonathan Buckley, Amy Douglas, Nancy Graham, Steve
Parker and Toby Spigel for their help in producing this book.

Illustrations by Brian Delf

CONTENTS

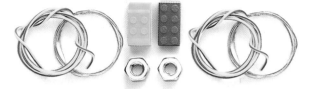

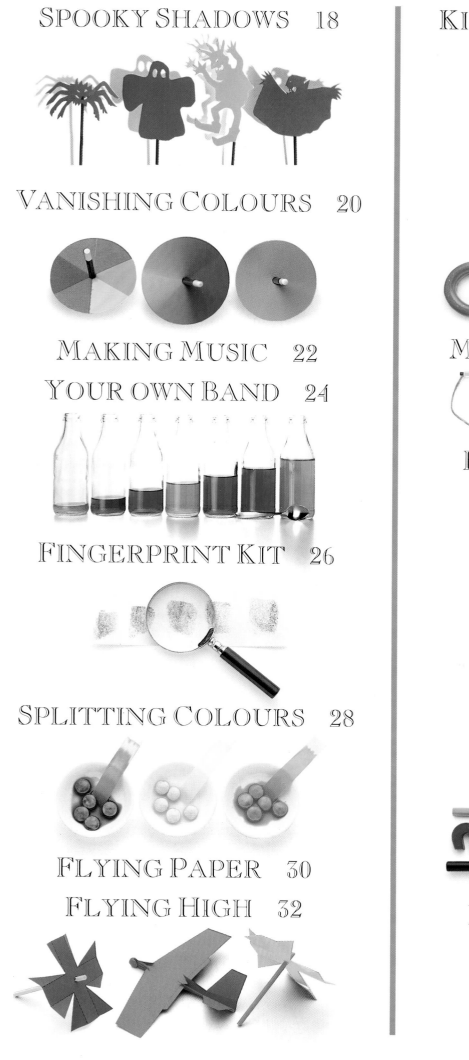

SCIENCE BY PICTURES

My First Science Book is full of fascinating experiments to do at home that will help you to find out more about why things happen the way they do in the world around you. Step-by-step photographs and simple instructions show you exactly what to do, and there are life-size photographs of everything you need to collect and of the finished projects. On the opposite page is a list of things to read before you start and below are the points to look for in each project.

How to use this book

The aim of the experiment
At the beginning of each experiment you can read exactly what the experiment is setting out to do.

The things you need
The things to collect for each experiment are shown life-size, to help you check you have everything you need.

Equipment
These illustrated checklists show you which equipment to have ready before you start an experiment.

KITCHEN CHEMISTRY

You don't need special powders and test tubes to be a chemist. Everything around you is made of chemicals and you can do all kinds of interesting tests on things around the kitchen. Here and on the next three pages you can find out how to test things to see if they are acid or alkaline.

You will need

Blotting paper

Half a lemon

Bicarbonate of soda

Water

Half a small red cabbage

Other things to test

Egg white

Cola drink

Milk of magnesia

Vinegar

A boiled sweet

A tomato

A slice of apple

Orange juice

Yogurt

Baking powder

Washing soda*

EQUIPMENT

Chopping board

Sieve

Bowl

Teaspoon

Small glasses or jars

Pen or pencil

Knife

Jug

Sticky labels

Notebook

The acid test

1 Chop up the cabbage and put it in a bowl. Pour hot water over it and leave it to soak until the water turns purple.

2 Hold the sieve over the jug. Pour the cabbage water into the jug through the sieve, so that the cabbage stays in the sieve.

3 Pour a little purple cabbage water into several of the small jars. Label one jar *Control* and put it to one side.

4 Pour a few drops of lemon juice into one of the other jars of purple cabbage water. Label the jar *Lemon juice*.

5 Mix a teaspoon of bicarbonate of soda with a little water. Stir it into a jar of purple water. Label it *Bicarbonate of soda*.

6 Do the same with all the other things you want to test. Label every jar to say what is in it as you do each test. Now turn the page.

54

55

*Wash your hands after handling washing soda

Things to remember

1 Read the instructions before you start and gather together everything you need for the experiment.

2 Put on an apron or old shirt and roll up your sleeves. Cover your work table with newspaper.

3 Follow the instructions carefully and only do one thing at a time.

4 Be very careful with sharp scissors. Do not use them unless an adult is there to help you.

5 Keep a record of each experiment and its results in your science notebook (see page 47).

6 When you have finished, put everything away, clean up any mess and wash your hands.

Step-by-step
Step-by-step photographs and clear instructions show you exactly what to do at each stage of the experiment.

Explanation
At the end of each experiment you will find a simple explanation of what has happened and why.

The final results
Life-size pictures show you what happens at the end of the experiment, so that you know what to expect.

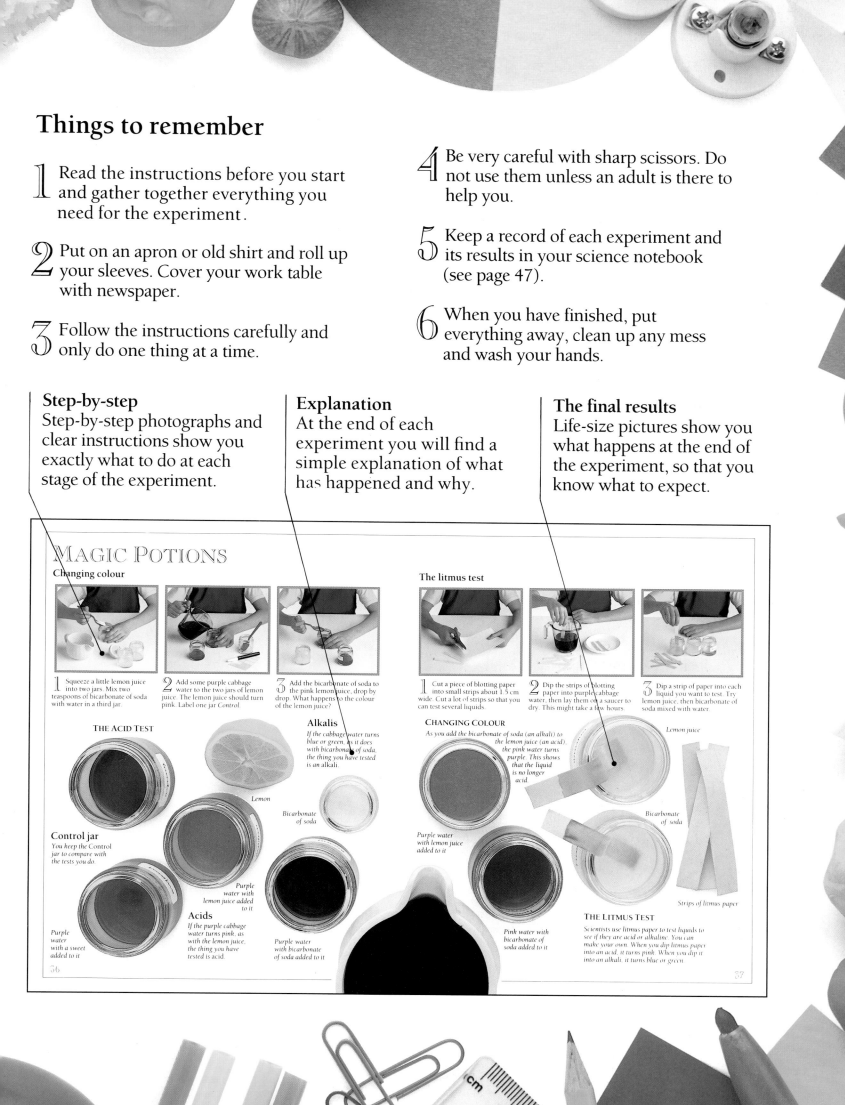

MAGIC POTIONS

Changing colour

1 Squeeze a little lemon juice into two jars. Mix two teaspoons of bicarbonate of soda with water in a third jar.

2 Add some purple cabbage water to the two jars of lemon juice. The lemon juice should turn pink. Label one jar *Control*.

3 Add the bicarbonate of soda to the pink lemon juice, drop by drop. What happens to the colour of the lemon juice?

THE ACID TEST

Alkalis
If the cabbage water turns blue or green, as it does with bicarbonate of soda, the thing you have tested is an alkali.

Lemon

Bicarbonate of soda

Control jar
You keep the Control jar to compare with the tests you do.

Purple water with lemon juice added to it

Acids
If the purple cabbage water turns pink, as with the lemon juice, the thing you have tested is acid.

Purple water with a sweet added to it

Purple water with bicarbonate of soda added to it

The litmus test

1 Cut a piece of blotting paper into small strips about 1.5 cm wide. Cut a lot of strips so that you can test several liquids.

2 Dip the strips of blotting paper into purple cabbage water, then lay them on a saucer to dry. This might take a few hours.

3 Dip a strip of paper into each liquid you want to test. Try lemon juice, then bicarbonate of soda mixed with water.

CHANGING COLOUR
As you add the bicarbonate of soda (an alkali) to the lemon juice (an acid), the pink water turns purple. This shows that the liquid is no longer acid

Lemon juice

Purple water with lemon juice added to it

Bicarbonate of soda

Pink water with bicarbonate of soda added to it

Strips of litmus paper

THE LITMUS TEST
Scientists use litmus paper to test liquids to see if they are acid or alkaline. You can make your own. When you dip litmus paper into an acid, it turns pink. When you dip it into an alkali, it turns blue or green

36

37

5

MAGIC BALLOONS

Some of the most interesting science experiments help you to see the effects of invisible forces at work around you. Strange things can happen to the most ordinary everyday objects. Here you can find out how to give balloons powers that seem magical.

A sheet of paper torn into small pieces

You will need

Balloons

Sugar

What to do

1 Blow up the balloons. You may need an adult to help you do this. Tie the end of each balloon into a firm knot.

2 Now rub each balloon hard against your sweater. The tricks work best if the sweater you are wearing is made of wool.

3 Hold one balloon just above the torn up pieces of paper. What happens? Then try holding a balloon just above some sugar.

"MAGICAL" ATTRACTION

The balloons pick up the torn up paper and sugar, as if by magic.

Electrical charges

Rubbing a balloon against wool charges it with static electricity. This gives the balloon enough magnetic power to pick up very light things, like the paper and sugar. It also makes the paper and sugar stick to the balloon.

Most things contain static electricity. You cannot see it, but you can rub it off one thing and on to another, making it static.

BOTTLE VOLCANO

Have you ever noticed that the first few sips of a hot drink always seem much hotter than the rest of the drink at the bottom of the cup? This simple experiment with water shows you in a dramatic way exactly what happens when you mix hot liquids and cold liquids together.

You will need

String

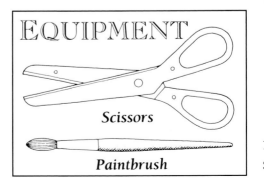

A large glass jar

A small bottle

Red food colouring or ink

EQUIPMENT

Scissors

Paintbrush

1 Cut a piece of string about 30 cm long. Tie one end of it firmly around the neck of the bottle, leaving the other end free.

2 Tie the other end of the string to the piece tied around the neck of the bottle, to make a loop of string for a handle.

3 Fill the large jar with cold water from a tap or jug. Don't fill it right to the top, as you need space to lower the bottle into it.

8

4 Fill the small bottle right up to the top with hot water. Stir in enough drops of food colouring to turn the water bright red.

5 Hold the small bottle by the string handle and lower it gently into the jar of cold water, being careful to keep it level.

VOLCANO IN A JAR

As you lower the small bottle into the jar of cold water, the hot water shoots up into the cold water like a volcano. Soon all the hot water will rise to the top of the jar.

Why hot water rises

When water is heated, it expands (takes up more space). This makes the hot water lighter than cold water, so it rises to the surface of the cold water.

On the Level

No two liquids are the same. Have you ever wondered why cream floats on top of milk, or why salad dressing separates into different layers? And did you know that some objects will sink in water but float on another liquid? Do this experiment and you can create a colourful giant cocktail and find out some fascinating things about different liquids at the same time.

You will need

Vegetable oil

Golden syrup

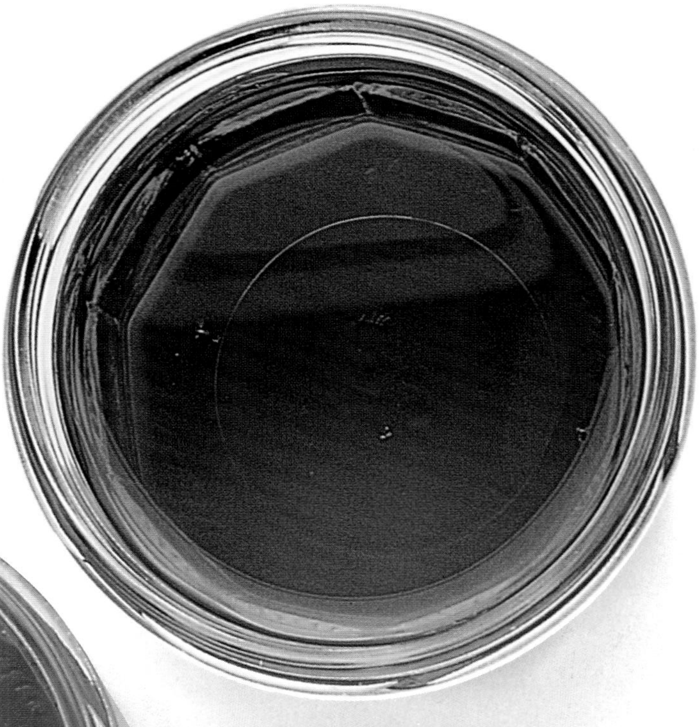

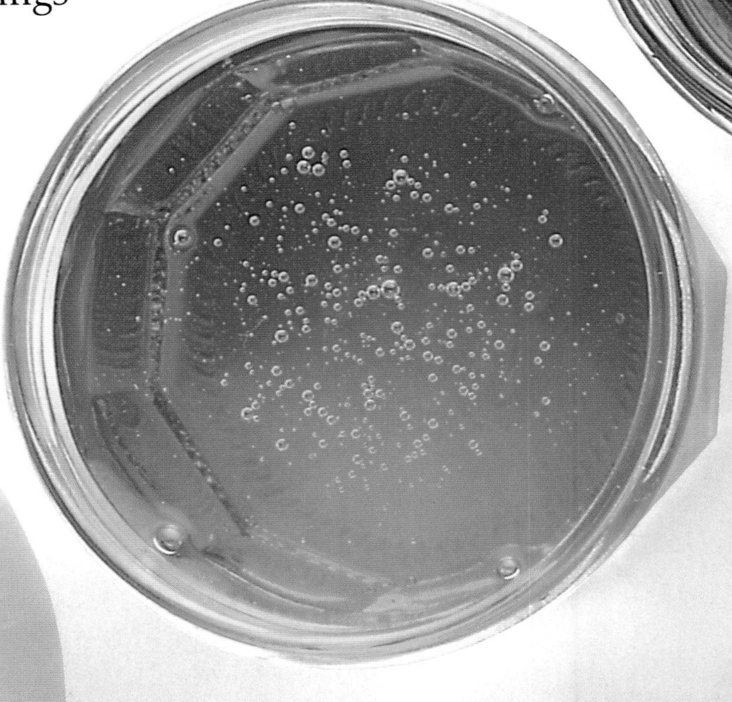

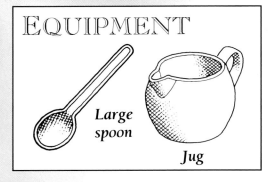

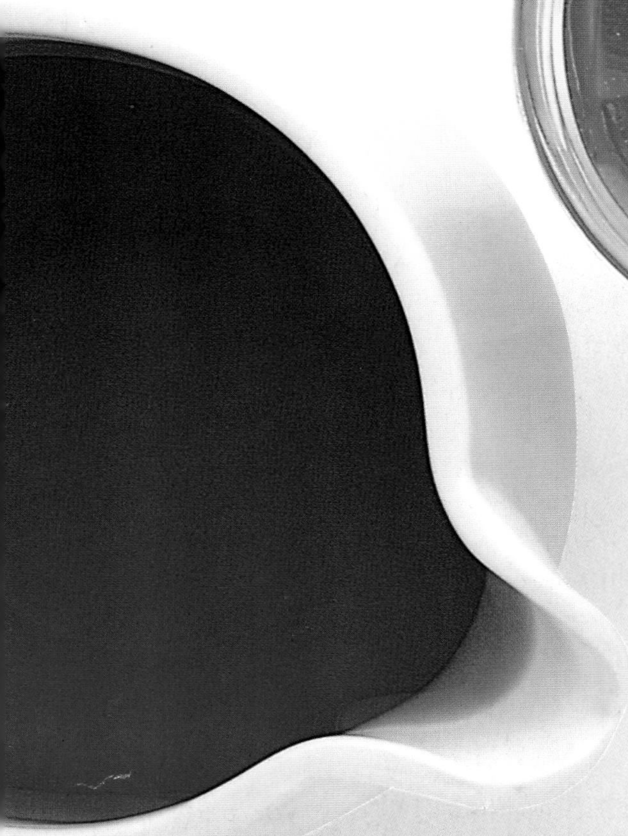

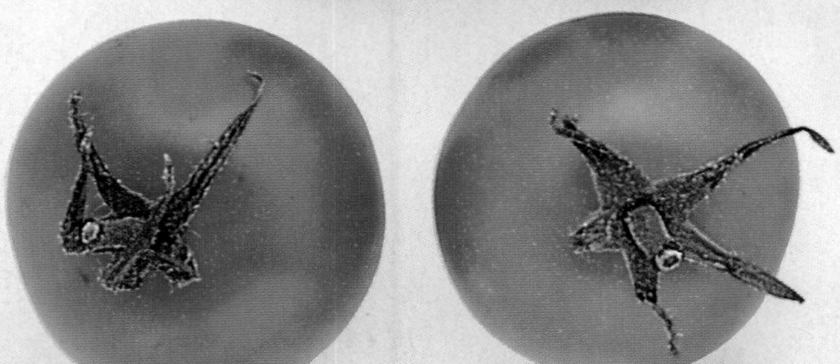

Water coloured with ink or food colouring

A large plastic container

Equipment

Large spoon

Jug

Things to float

Nuts

Plastic toys

Small tomatoes

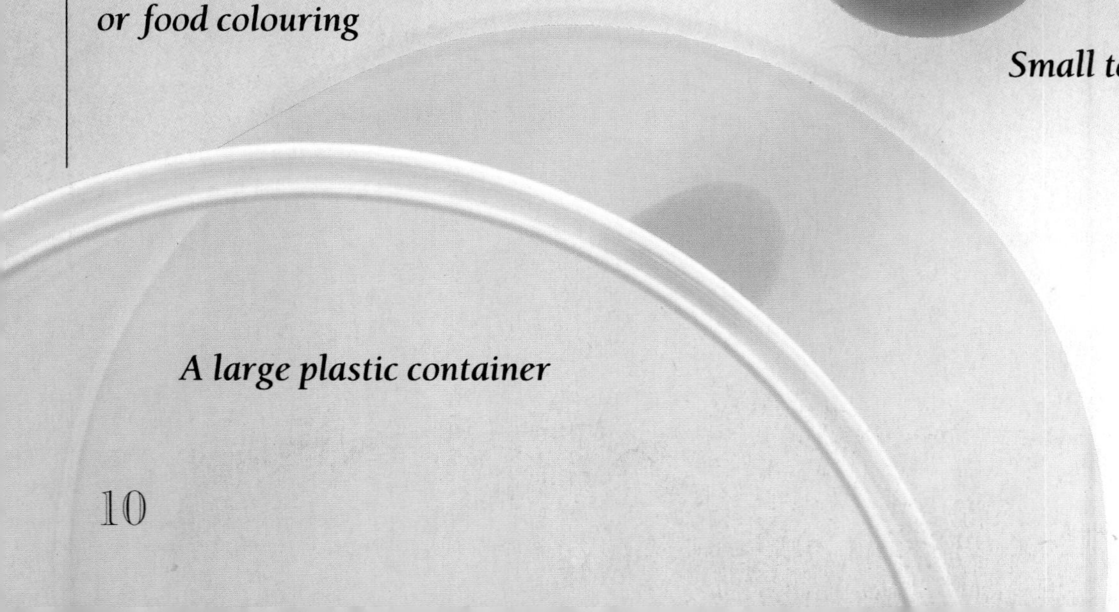

Small metal objects

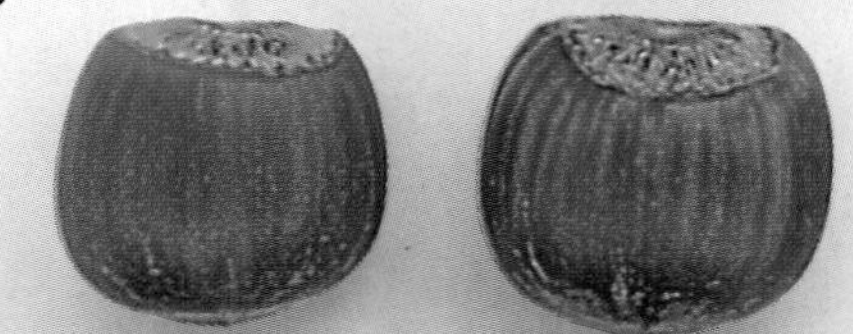

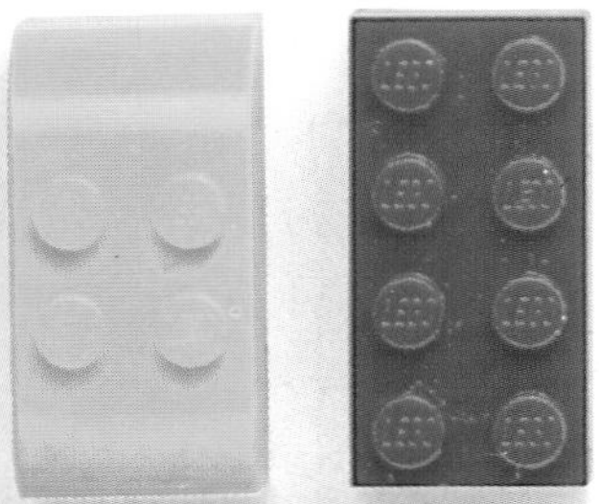

Dried pasta

Grapes

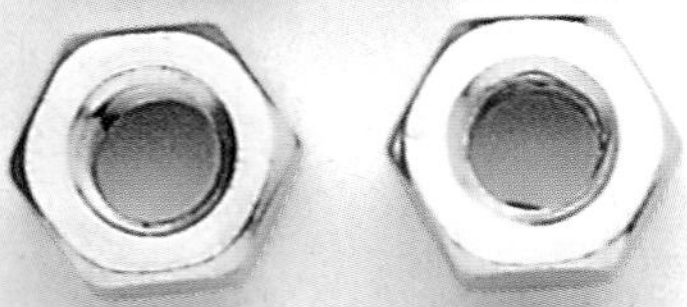

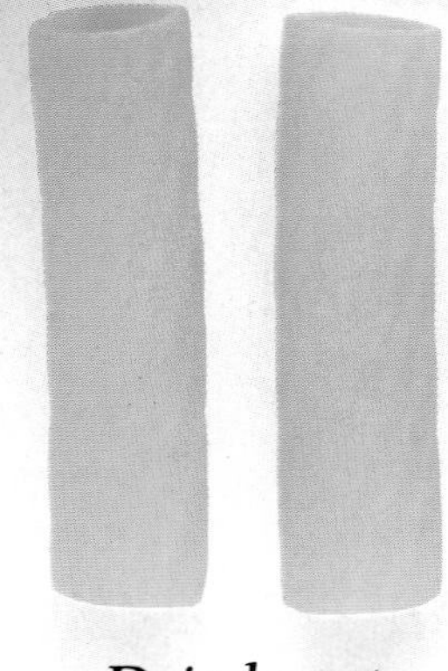

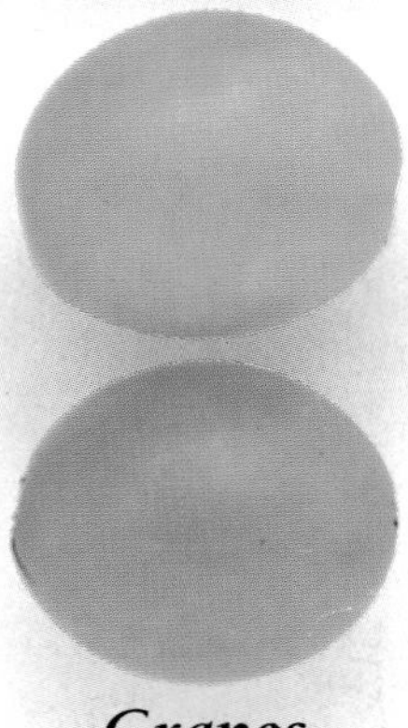

What to do

1 Carefully pour golden syrup into the container over the back of the spoon, until the container is a quarter full.

2 Slowly pour the same amount of vegetable oil into the container. Then add the same amount again of coloured water.

3 Wait until the liquids have settled into layers. Then gently drop different objects into the container, to see what floats.

LIQUID COCKTAIL

The liquids separate into three layers, with the syrup on the bottom, the water above that and the oil on top of the water.
Liquids do this because some of them are lighter or less dense than others. A lighter liquid will float on top of a heavier or more dense liquid.

Floaters and sinkers

Some of the objects you drop into the container will sink. Others will float at different levels, depending on how heavy they are. Objects float best in dense liquids, as these support their weight best.

11

MULTI-COLOURED FLOWERS

Why do we put flowers in a vase of water and where does the water in the vase go? In this clever experiment you use food colouring or ink to reveal something that you would normally never see: how flowers drink and where the water goes.

You will need

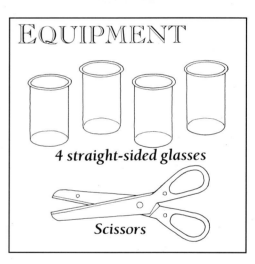

White carnations

Jug of water

Different coloured inks or food dyes

EQUIPMENT

4 straight-sided glasses

Scissors

What to do

1 Pour about 2 cm of different-coloured food colouring or ink into each glass. Add about 2 cm of water to each glass.

2 Trim the flower stems to 5 cm taller than the glasses. Cut along the stems of two flowers, to split them in half lengthwise.

3 Stand a flower in each glass of water. Stand each half of the two split-stemmed flowers in different coloured water.

12

Red flower

Blue flower

Pink flower

Green flower

Tiny veins

Look closely at the flowers and you will see the tiny veins that carry water to each part of the flower petals. They have been stained by the food colouring.

Colour change

Leave the flowers in a warm room for a few hours and they will slowly turn the same colour as the water in which they are standing.

Pink and blue flower

Red and green flower

Two-tone flowers

Each half of the flowers with the split stems will turn the same colour as the water in which that half of the stem is standing. This shows that the tiny tubes for water in each part of the flower stem lead to a specific part of the flower.

13

WEATHER STATION

Set up your own weather station and you will be able to keep a record of your local weather. Here and overleaf you can find out how to make a rain gauge, for measuring rainfall, a barometer, to show changes in the air pressure and a wind vane, so that you know which way the wind is blowing.

You will need

Food colouring or ink

Waterproof sticky tape

A glue stick

A short pencil with an eraser on the end

Three long pencils

A drinking straw

A shallow bowl

EQUIPMENT

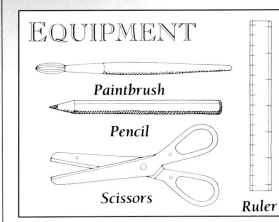

Paintbrush

Pencil

Scissors

Ruler

A yogurt pot

A large, straight-sided plastic bottle

14

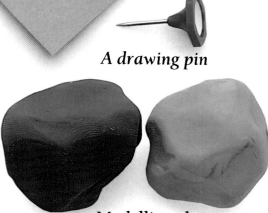

Thin card

A drawing pin

Modelling clay

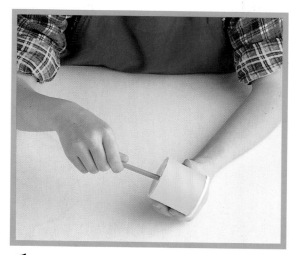

Making the wind vane

1 Make a hole in the centre of the base of the yogurt pot. Push the short pencil into it, so the eraser end sticks out as shown.

2 Cut four small triangles out of thin card. Then cut out a triangle about 3 cm deep and a bigger one about 5 cm deep.

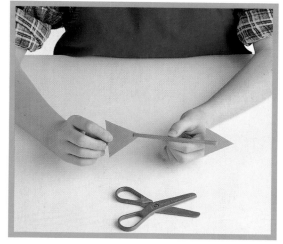

3 Glue the four small triangles to the base of the yogurt pot, so that they point in four different directions, as shown.

4 Cut 1 cm slits at both sides of each end of the straw. Slot the two big triangles into them, pointing in the same direction.

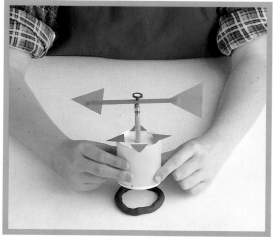

5 Push the drawing pin through the centre of the straw**. Then stick the pin into the eraser. Make sure the vane can spin easily.

6 Make a sausage of modelling clay and bend it into a ring. Push the clay around the base of the wind vane.

A narrow, clear plastic bottle*

* Use the narrowest bottle you can find.

** Ask an adult to help you.

15

WEATHER WATCH

Making the rain gauge

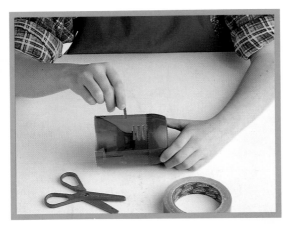

1 Cut off the top quarter of the large plastic bottle, using the scissors. Ask an adult to help you make the first cut.

2 Slide the top of the bottle upside down into the base of the bottle, to act as a funnel. Tape the edges together, as shown.

3 Cut tiny strips of sticky tape. Tape them to the side of the bottle about a centimetre apart, to act as a measuring scale.

Making the barometer

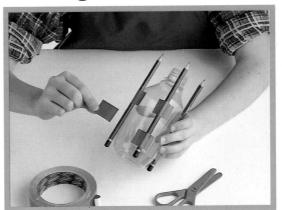

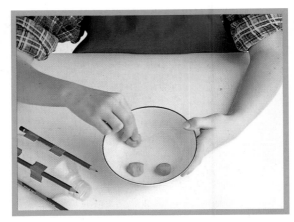

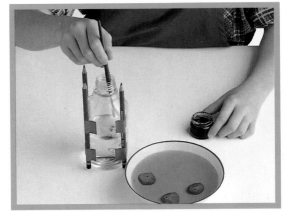

1 Tape three long pencils to the small plastic bottle. The points of the pencils should stick out above the top of the bottle.

2 Using the bottle to help you, stick three lumps of modelling clay to the bottom of the bowl, for the pencils to go into.

3 Half fill both the bowl and the bottle with water. Add a few drops of food colouring or ink to the water with the paintbrush.

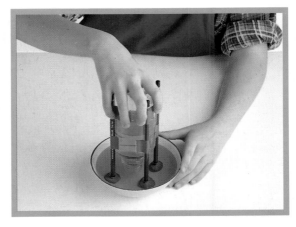

4 Cover the top of the bottle with your hand. Turn it upside down and lower it under the water in the bowl.

5 Take your hand away from the mouth of the bottle. Keeping the bottle straight, push the pencils firmly into the modelling clay.

6 Cut tiny strips of sticky tape. Tape them to the side of the bottle to make a scale, as when making the rain gauge.

RECORDING THE WEATHER

Stand your wind vane and rain gauge outside. Keep the barometer indoors, away from direct sunlight. Check your weather station every day and make a record of any changes in your science notebook. As well as reading the instruments you have made, write down how many hours of rain or sun there have been and note what sort of clouds are in the sky.

How the barometer works

A barometer measures air pressure. Air presses down on the water in the bowl. When the air pressure rises, the air pushes down harder on the water, making the water in the bottle rise higher up the scale. When the air pressure drops, the water level in the bottle drops lower.

The water level will only rise or drop slightly, so check it very carefully.

If your rain gauge has a plastic base, fill the base with water before putting the rain gauge outside.

Measuring the rainfall

When it rains, check every day how far up the scale the water comes. Make a note of the reading, then empty the rain gauge.

Which way is the wind blowing?

Stand the wind vane outside on a flat surface. Use a compass to position it so that one of the triangles points north. Mark the triangles north, south, east and west. Write down which direction the wind is blowing from. The north wind, for example, blows from north to south.

17

SPOOKY SHADOWS

Make some scary puppets and entertain your friends to a spine-chilling shadow puppet theatre. Below are some puppet patterns to trace and opposite you can see how to make and operate the puppets.

Tracing paper

Thin card

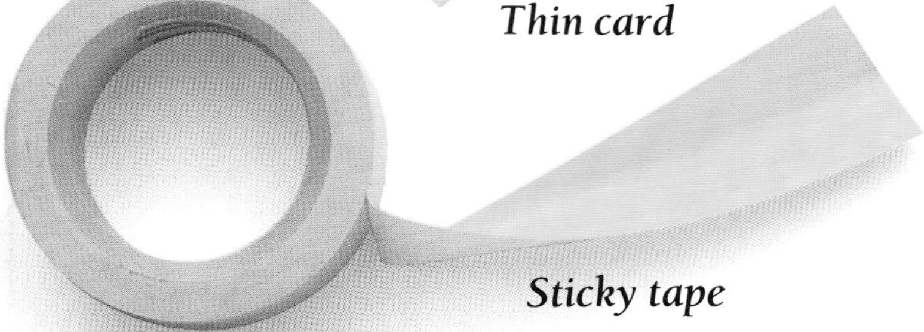

You will need

Sticky tape

Thin sticks

A strong torch

EQUIPMENT

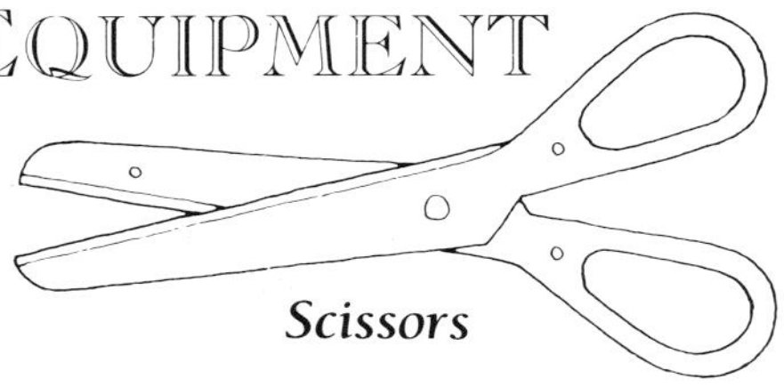

Scissors

Pencil

Puppet patterns

Vicious vampire

Terrifying tarantula

Scary spectre

Ghastly ghoul

18

Making the puppets

1 Trace the puppet patterns from the book on to tracing paper. (Or make up your own puppets and draw them on to card.)

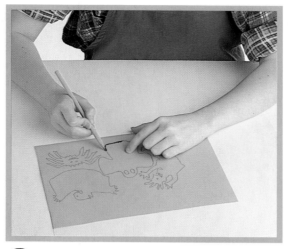

2 Lay the tracing paper wrong side down on card. Scribble over the back of the lines you traced, to transfer them to the card.

3 Carefully cut the puppets out of the card. You can use a pencil to make holes for eyes. Tape each puppet to the end of a stick.

SHADOW THEATRE

You need two people to set up the theatre: one to hold the torch and the other to work the puppets. Make sure the room is dark, then shine the torch at the wall and move the puppets around between the torch and the wall. With practice, you can make the shadows grow bigger and even change shape.

Monster shadows

Light rays are straight. So the closer a puppet is to the torch, the more light it blocks and the bigger the shadow.

19

VANISHING COLOURS

Light looks white, but it is really made of rainbow colours. Make this simple multi-coloured wheel and you will be able to make colours disappear, then appear again, as if by magic. Where do the colours go and why? Spin the wheel, then read about what happens at the bottom of the page opposite.

You will need

Thin card

A short, sharp pencil

A glue stick

Tracing paper

Coloured paper (red, orange, yellow, green, blue and purple)

Making the colour wheel

EQUIPMENT

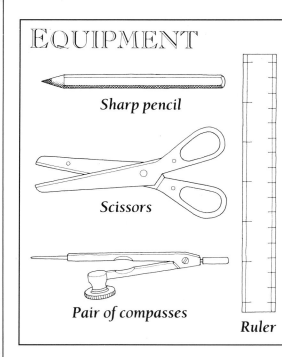

Sharp pencil

Scissors

Pair of compasses

Ruler

1 Open the compasses to 5 cm and draw a circle on the card. Then mark six points, 5 cm apart, around the circle with the compasses.

2 Join each pair of opposite points together, so the three lines cross in the centre of the circle. Cut out the circle.

3 Trace a segment of the circle. Glue it on to card and cut it out. Draw round the shape on each colour of paper and cut it out.

4 Glue the pieces of coloured paper to the circle of card in this order: red, orange, yellow, green, blue and purple.

5 Punch a hole in the centre of the circle with the tip of the scissors. Push the pencil through the hole, as shown.

SPINNING COLOURS

Spin the colour wheel fast and watch what happens. Which colour or colours can you see? When the wheel spins fast, your eyes and brain working together cannot see each colour separately, so the colours blur together to make a different colour.

As the colour wheel slows down, the blurring lessens, and your eyes and brain can pick out the different colours again. Try making other wheels in just two or three colours. Do you always see the same colour when you spin them?

21

MAKING MUSIC

Why do things make noises? There are noises all around you all of the time, but you cannot see them. Try making your own musical instruments though and you will not only have lots of fun, but will also learn a lot about how sounds are made at the same time. Here you can find out how to make a harp from elastic bands, a xylophone from bottles and pan pipes from drinking straws. Turn the page to see the finished instruments, then start twanging, banging and blowing!

You will need

A glue stick

8 plastic drinking straws

A metal spoon

Food colouring or ink

Water

Several glass bottles the same size

**2 strips of card
14 cm by 2.5 cm**

*Thick elastic
bands*

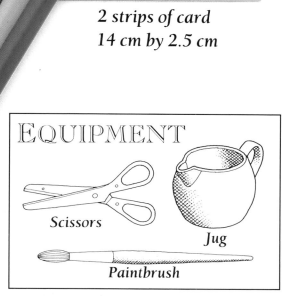

*A baking tin
or plastic box*

Making the pan pipes

1 Spread glue along one strip of card. Glue the eight straws to the card at equal distances, with the tops of the straws in line.

2 Glue the second strip of card over the top of the straws. Trim the straws so that each one is shorter than the one before.

Making the harp

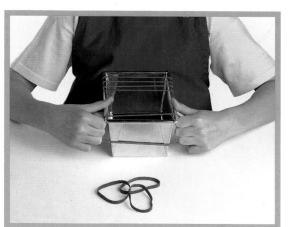

1 Stretch eight elastic bands around the baking tin or plastic box as shown, so that they are all the same distance apart.

2 To give the elastic bands different notes, tighten each one by pulling it and catching it on the edge of the tin.

Making the xylophone

1 Stand the bottles in a row. Pour water into them, so that each bottle contains a little more water than the one before.

2 To make the xylophone look prettier, add a few drops of food colouring to each bottle of water and stir it in.

YOUR OWN BAND

Now that you have made your musical instruments, see if you can play a tune on any of them. The instruments shown here are plucked, blown and banged upon, but each of them really makes sounds in the same way. All sounds, both nice and nasty, are carried by the air around you. When you play a musical instrument, it makes the air around it vibrate. The air carries this vibration to your ears. Your eardrums vibrate and you hear the sound made by the instrument.

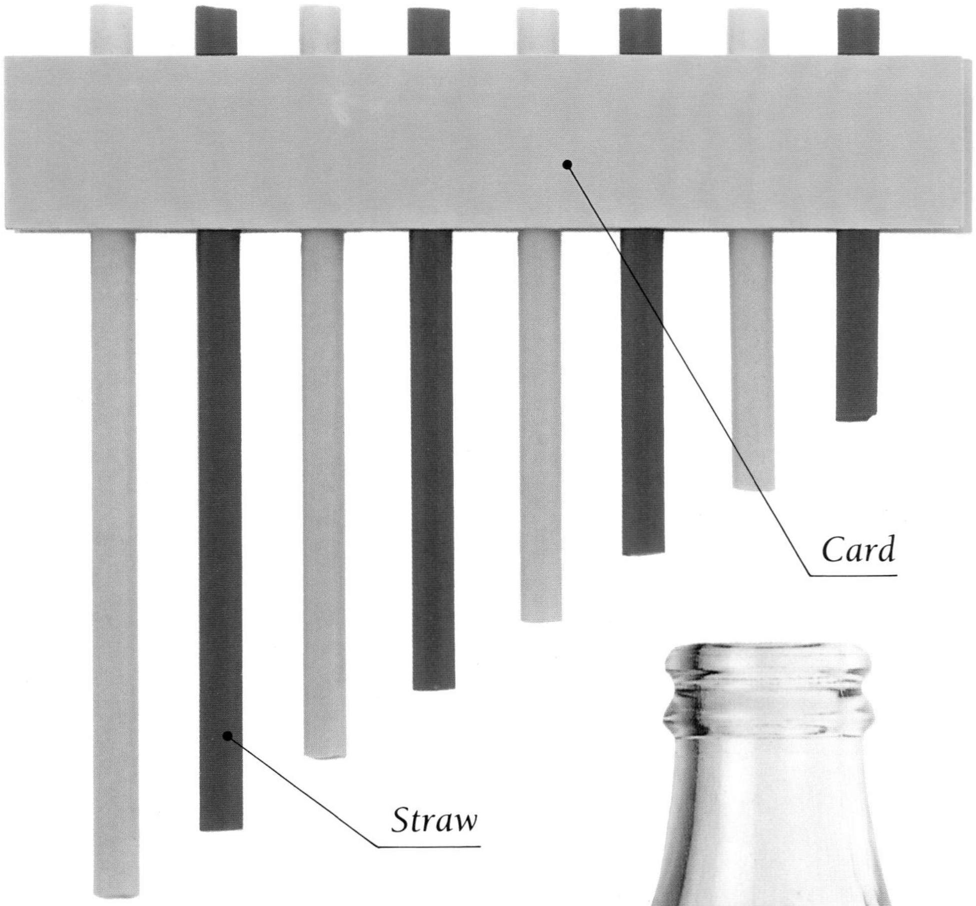

Card

Straw

PAN PIPES

The pipes are a simple wind instrument. Hold them to your mouth with the straws pointing downwards, as shown here, and blow across the tops of the straws. You will hear quiet, flute-like sounds. The shorter the straws are, the higher the notes they make.

BOTTLE XYLOPHONE

The xylophone forms the percussion part of your band. Tap each bottle in turn with the spoon to see what note it makes. The more water there is in the bottle, the shorter the column of air that vibrates in the bottle and the higher the sound it makes.

If you adjust the amount of water in the bottles, you should find that you can play part of a musical scale by striking each one in turn.

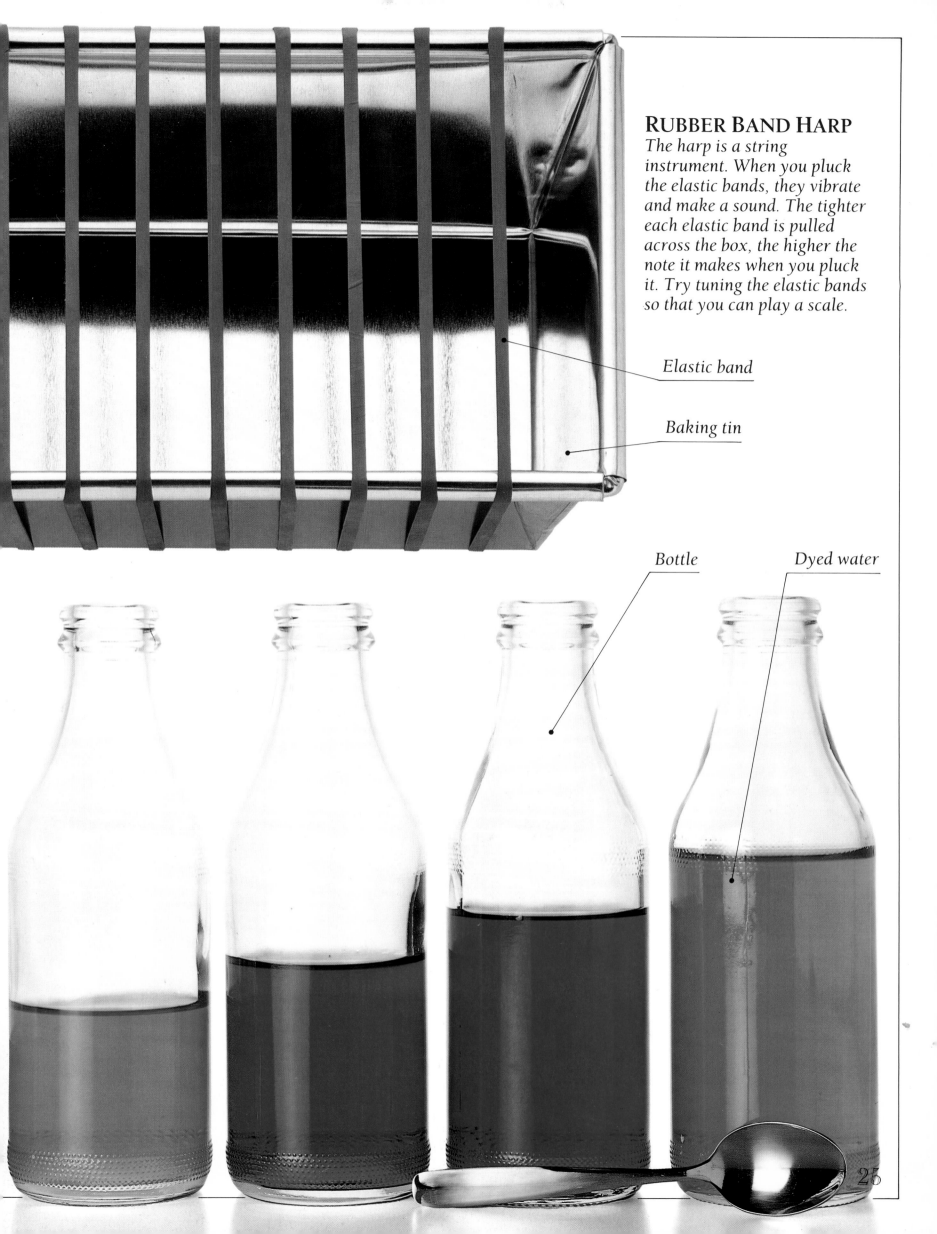

RUBBER BAND HARP

The harp is a string instrument. When you pluck the elastic bands, they vibrate and make a sound. The tighter each elastic band is pulled across the box, the higher the note it makes when you pluck it. Try tuning the elastic bands so that you can play a scale.

Elastic band

Baking tin

Bottle

Dyed water

25

FINGERPRINT KIT

No two people have the same fingerprints. This makes them valuable clues when detectives are investigating a crime. Fingerprints are usually invisible, but detectives use scientific methods to reveal fingerprints found at the scene of a crime and compare them with suspects' fingerprints. Read what to do below and you can do some detective work of your own.

You will need

Talcum powder

White paper

A small magnifying glass

A stamp pad

A fine paintbrush

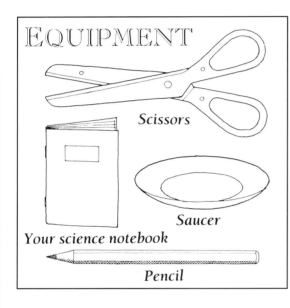

EQUIPMENT

Scissors

Saucer

Your science notebook

Pencil

Taking fingerprints

1 Press the pad of one of the suspect's fingers lightly on the stamp pad. Roll it from side to side, to cover it with ink.

2 Press the suspect's finger firmly on a piece of paper. Hold it as shown in the picture and roll it from side to side.

3 Take prints of all the suspect's fingers and label them. Then examine them carefully. Are all the prints the same?

26

Dusting for fingerprints

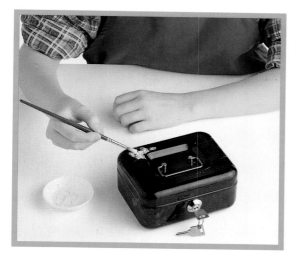

1 Pour some talcum powder into a saucer. Dust the talcum powder lightly on something hard and shiny that people often touch*.

2 Blow gently on the places that you have powdered. Most of the powder will blow away, except where there are greasy marks.

3 Now brush the powdered spots very lightly with a fine paintbrush. Any fingerprints will gradually appear, as if by magic.

FINGERPRINT FILE

When you have taken all the suspects' fingerprints, cut them out and glue them into your science notebook. Then you can compare them with any fingerprints you find around your home.

Use a magnifying glass to study the details of fingerprints.

Suspect's fingerprint

Fingerprint found on cash box

* The edges of windows, door knobs and light switches are good places to try.

SPLITTING COLOURS

Many of the inks and dyes that are used to colour things are really mixtures of several different coloured chemicals or *pigments*. The two experiments here show you how to separate the different coloured pigments in felt-tip pens and the food colouring used in sweets.

You will need

White blotting paper

Coloured felt-tip pens

Smarties

Half a teaspoon of salt

EQUIPMENT

Glass or jam jar   *Jug of water*

Scissors

Saucers

Felt-tip pen test

1 Cut out a rectangle of blotting paper big enough to roll into a tube that you can slide into the glass you are going to use.

2 Make blobs of different colours* about 4 cm from the bottom of the blotting paper with the felt-tip pens.

3 Pour a little water into the glass and stir in the salt. Roll the blotting paper into a tube and stand it in the glass.

* *Dark colours are the most interesting colours to test.*

Smartie test

1 Choose three colours to test. Put five or six sweets the same colour in each saucer. Add a few drops of water to them.

2 Turn the sweets over and stir them round a little, so that most of the colour runs off them and colours the water.

3 Cut three strips of blotting paper. Lay a strip into each of the saucers as shown, with one end in the coloured water.

FELT-TIP PEN TEST

As the water rises up the blotting paper, it dissolves the pigments in the ink blots and carries them up with it. The different pigments move up the paper at different speeds, so they separate and you can see bands of different colours.

SMARTIE TEST

The pigments used on the sweets are absorbed by the blotting paper in the same way as the pigments in the felt-tip pens. As they move up the blotting paper, they separate. Some of the colours only contain one pigment.

29

FLYING PAPER

How do aeroplanes fly? Launch a piece of paper into the air and it will just swoop down to the ground. But if you make a plane with the piece of paper, it will fly really well.

Here and on the next three pages you can find out how to make an amazing superglider and helicopter. They are not only fun to make and play with, but will also teach you a lot about how things fly.

You will need

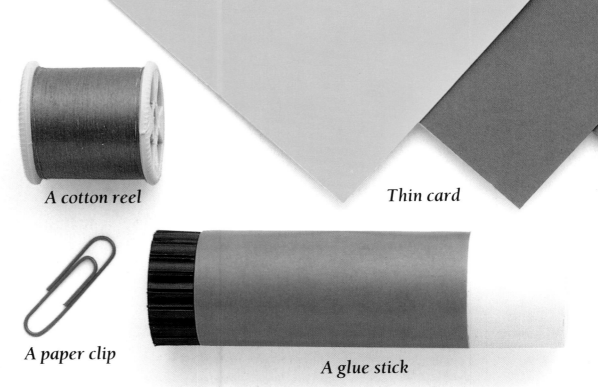

A cotton reel

Thin card

A paper clip

A glue stick

A drinking straw 13 cm long

Tracing paper

A small lump of modelling clay

String

EQUIPMENT

Scissors

Ruler

Pencil

HELICOPTER PATTERN

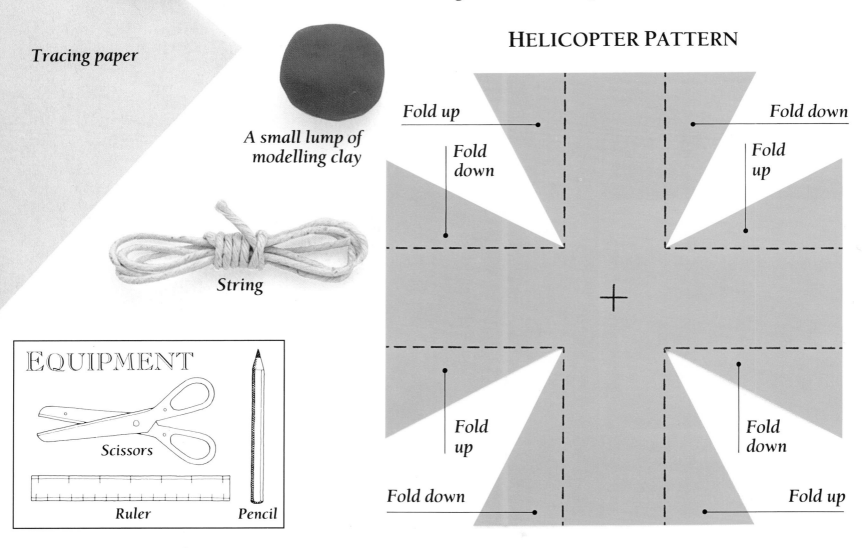

Fold up

Fold down

Fold down

Fold up

Fold up

Fold down

Fold down

Fold up

SUPERGLIDER PATTERN

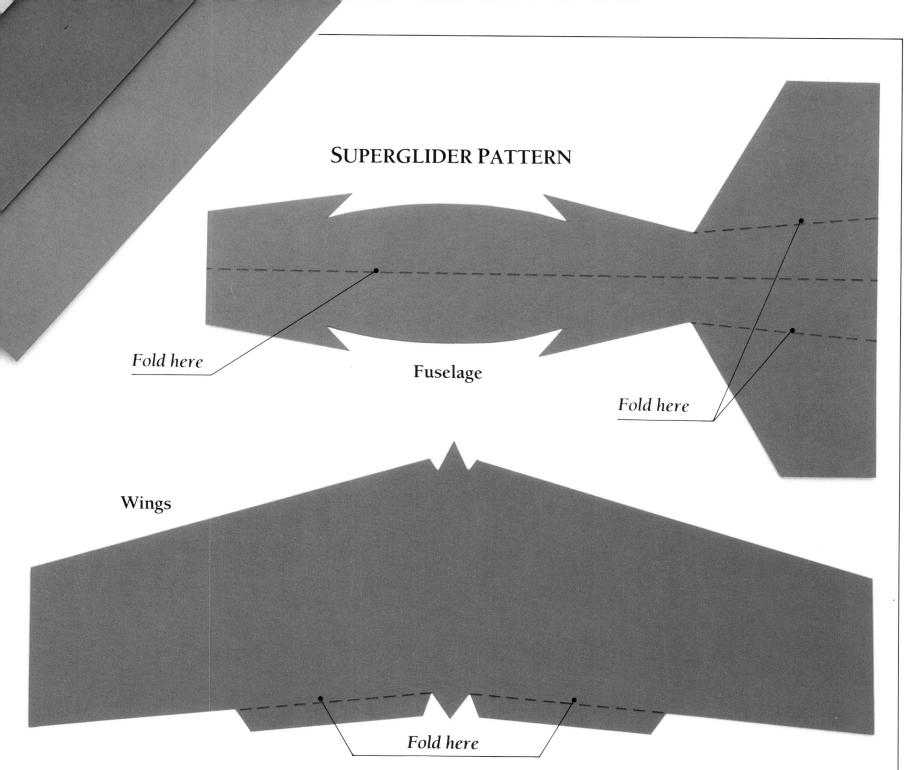

Fold here

Fuselage

Fold here

Wings

Fold here

Making the superglider

1 Trace the outlines of the two superglider pattern pieces onto tracing paper. Trace along the fold lines using dotted lines.

2 Turn the tracing paper over. Lay it on the card and scribble over the lines you have traced, to transfer the pattern to the card.

3 Cut the wings and fuselage out of the card. Score along the fold lines, using your ruler and the point of your scissors *.

* This helps to make the folds sharper.   *Now turn the page.*

FLYING HIGH

Superglider (continued)

4 Fold the fuselage in half along the fold line, then open it out again. Fold down the two tail fins and the two wing flaps.

5 Slot the back of the wings into the back notches on the fuselage. Slot the front of the wings into the front two notches.

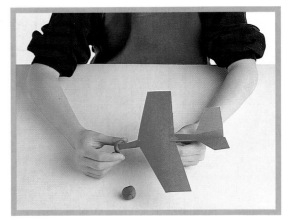

6 Put the paper clip on the nose of the aeroplane. Fold a piece of modelling clay around the paper clip, to act as a weight.

Making the helicopter

1 Trace the pattern for the helicopter rotor on to tracing paper. Trace the fold lines, using dotted lines.

2 Turn the tracing paper over. Lay it on the card and scribble over the lines you have traced, to transfer the pattern to the card.

3 Cut the helicopter rotor out of the card. Score along the fold lines, using your ruler and the point of your scissors.

4 Each rotor blade has two fold lines. Fold one side of each rotor blade up and the other side down, along the fold lines.

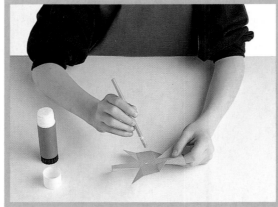

5 Make a hole in the middle of the rotor. Spread glue around one end of the straw. Push the straw through the hole in the rotor.

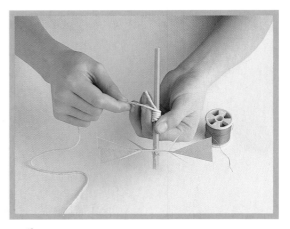

6 Make a loop in one end of the string. Wind string anti-clockwise over the loop around the straw beneath the rotor.

Helicopter launch

Push the straw into the cotton reel. Hold the cotton reel in one hand and pull the string hard with the other.

As the helicopter rotors spin, they push air down, squashing the air under the rotors. The pressure of this air pushes the helicopter into the air.

Taking off

To launch the superglider, hold it just behind the nose and let it go gently. The plane flies because the shape of the wings makes the air flow faster over the wings than below them. The pressure of air below the wing is greater than it is above the wing, helping to keep the plane airborne for longer.

If the superglider keeps tipping upwards and then diving, try adding a little more modelling clay to the nose. If the glider dives too fast, the nose may be too heavy, so remove some modelling clay.

KITCHEN CHEMISTRY

You don't need special powders and test tubes to be a chemist. Everything around you is made of chemicals and you can do all kinds of interesting tests on things around the kitchen. Here and on the next three pages you can find out how to test things to see if they are acid or alkaline.

Blotting paper

Half a lemon

Bicarbonate of soda

You will need

Water

Half a small red cabbage

The acid test

1 Chop up the cabbage and put it in a bowl. Pour hot water over it and leave it to soak until the water turns purple.

2 Hold the sieve over the jug. Pour the cabbage water into the jug through the sieve, so that the cabbage stays in the sieve.

3 Pour a little purple cabbage water into several of the small jars. Label one jar *Control* and put it to one side.

Other things to test

Egg white

Cola drink

Milk of magnesia

Vinegar

Orange juice

Yogurt

A boiled sweet

A tomato

A slice of apple

Baking powder

Washing soda*

EQUIPMENT

Sieve

Bowl

Chopping board

Teaspoon

Pen or pencil

Knife

Jug

Small glasses or jars

Sticky labels

Notebook

4 Pour a few drops of lemon juice into one of the other jars of purple cabbage water. Label the jar *Lemon juice*.

5 Mix a teaspoon of bicarbonate of soda with a little water. Stir it into a jar of purple water. Label it *Bicarbonate of soda*.

6 Do the same with all the other things you want to test. Label every jar to say what is in it as you do each test. Now turn the page.

*Wash your hands after handling washing soda

35

MAGIC POTIONS

Changing colour

1 Squeeze a little lemon juice into two jars. Mix two teaspoons of bicarbonate of soda with water in a third jar.

2 Add some purple cabbage water to the two jars of lemon juice. The lemon juice should turn pink. Label one jar *Control*.

3 Add the bicarbonate of soda to the pink lemon juice, drop by drop. What happens to the colour of the lemon juice?

THE ACID TEST

Alkalis

If the cabbage water turns blue or green, as it does with bicarbonate of soda, the thing you have tested is an alkali.

Lemon

Bicarbonate of soda

Control jar

You keep the Control jar to compare with the tests you do.

Purple water with lemon juice added to it

Acids

If the purple cabbage water turns pink, as with the lemon juice, the thing you have tested is acid.

Purple water with a sweet added to it

Purple water with bicarbonate of soda added to it

The litmus test

1 Cut a piece of blotting paper into small strips about 1.5 cm wide. Cut a lot of strips so that you can test several liquids.

2 Dip the strips of blotting paper into purple cabbage water, then lay them on a saucer to dry. This might take a few hours.

3 Dip a strip of paper into each liquid you want to test. Try lemon juice, then bicarbonate of soda mixed with water.

CHANGING COLOUR

As you add the bicarbonate of soda (an alkali) to the lemon juice (an acid), the pink water turns purple. This shows that the liquid is no longer acid.

Lemon juice

Purple water with lemon juice added to it

Bicarbonate of soda

Pink water with bicarbonate of soda added to it

Strips of litmus paper

THE LITMUS TEST

Scientists use litmus paper to test liquids to see if they are acid or alkaline. You can make your own. When you dip litmus paper into an acid, it turns pink. When you dip it into an alkali, it turns blue or green.

MAGNET TRICKS

Magnets have strange powers and can draw some things to them as if by magic. You cannot see how a magnet works, but you can find out more about it by trying out the magnet tests and tricks shown here. Then turn the page to see how to set up a clever magnet game.

You will need

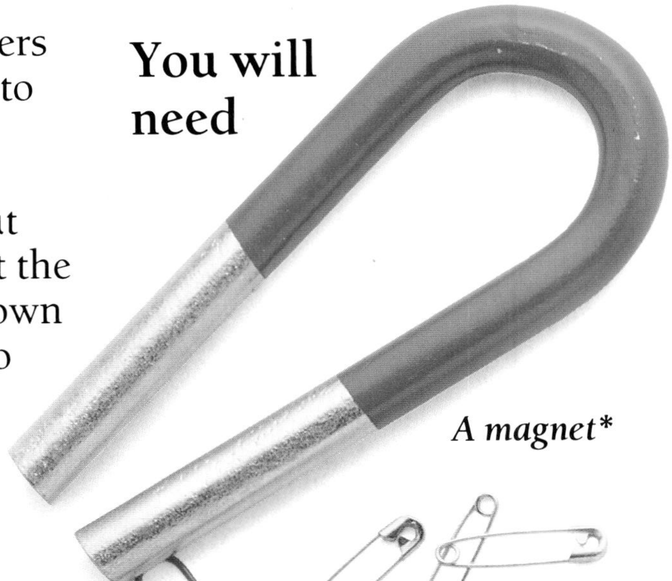

A magnet*

For the magnet tests

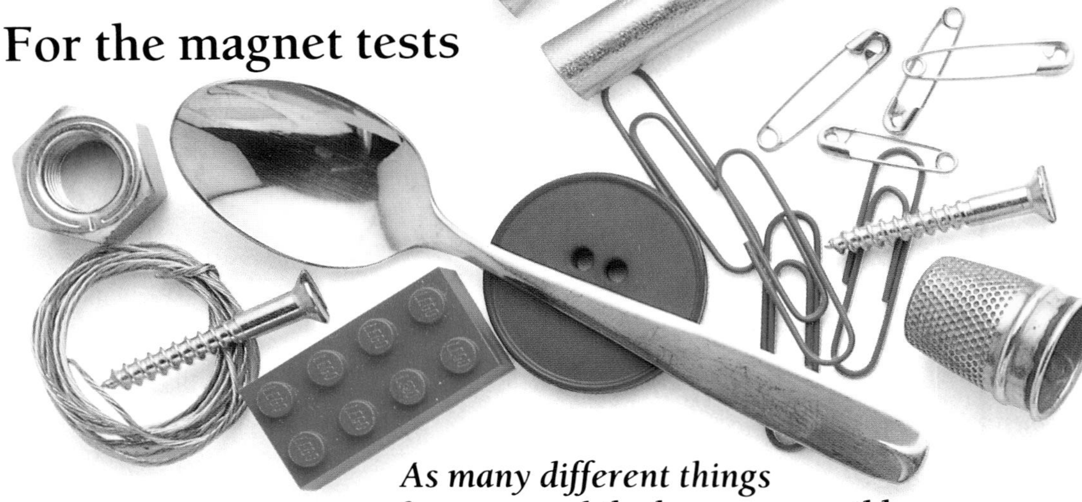

As many different things from around the home as possible

For the compass and floating needles

Small pieces of paper

2 darning needles

A shallow bowl of water

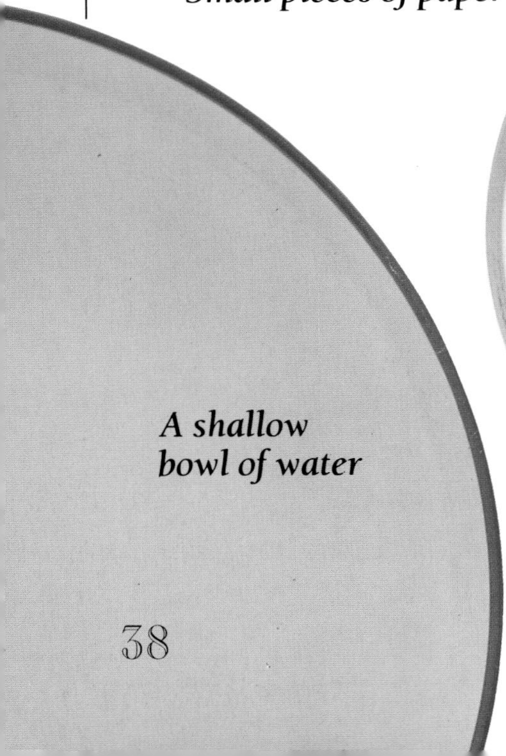

A glass of water

Magnet tests

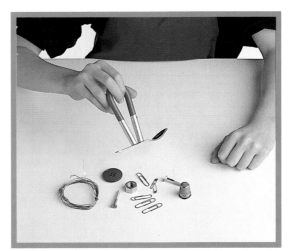

1 Test your magnet on things around the room and the objects you have collected. Which things does it pick up?

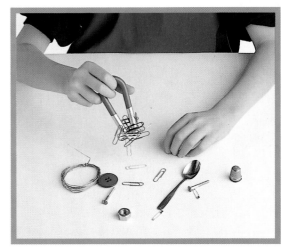

2 How strong is your magnet? How many paper clips can it pick up? Can you pick them up by holding the magnet above them?

3 Do magnets work through glass? Drop a paper clip in a glass of water. Can you slide it up the glass with a magnet?

* You can buy magnets at hardware shops.

Making magnets

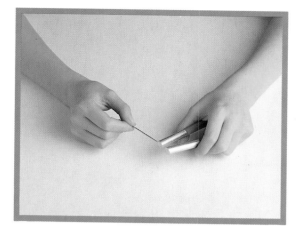

You can turn a darning needle into a magnet. Just stroke it about twenty times in the same direction with one end of your magnet.

Making a compass

Magnetize a darning needle, as shown above. Float a small piece of paper on water in a glass and lay the needle on top of it.

Pushing and pulling

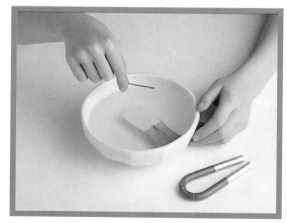

Magnetize two needles and lay them close together on pieces of paper floating in a bowl of water. What happens?

Finding North

The piece of paper turns until one end of the needle points North. The Earth is like a giant magnet and the magnetized needle acts like a compass needle.

Floating needles

The pieces of paper turn as two ends of the magnetic needles pull towards each other. The two ends of a magnet are different. One end pulls one end of another magnet to it, but pushes away the other end of the second magnet.

MAGNETIC FISHING

Set up this unusual fishing game and compete with your friends to see who has the mightiest magnet and can catch the most fish in the shortest time. You need a magnet for each player*, so the more magnets you have, the more people can play the game.

You will need

A magnet for each person playing

Lots of paper clips

Sticky tape

Scissors

String

A small stick for each player

A large bowl of water

Aluminium foil

* You can buy magnets at hardware shops.

Setting up the game

1 Fold the aluminium foil in half, then in half again. Cut fishes out of the folded foil, using the first fish as a pattern piece.

2 Slide a paper clip onto the front end of each aluminium foil fish. Drop all the fish into the bowl of water.

3 Cut pieces of string about 20 cm long. Tie a magnet to one end of each piece. Tie the other end to a stick and tape it down.

How to play

Catch the fish by picking them up with the magnets. If two players catch the same fish, they must put it back in the bowl. The player who catches the most fish is the winner.

ELECTRICAL FUN

Electricity is one of the most mysterious sources of power, yet it runs the lights in your home and many everyday household machines. The electricity that runs through wires is called current electricity. You can find out more about how it works by making a simple circuit run on a battery, which provides a small, safe amount of electricity. Below you can see how to make the circuit and over the page you can find out how to turn a circuit into a good game.

★ *Electricity from the mains is very dangerous. Never touch or play with electric plugs, sockets, fires or machines.*

You will need
For the simple circuit

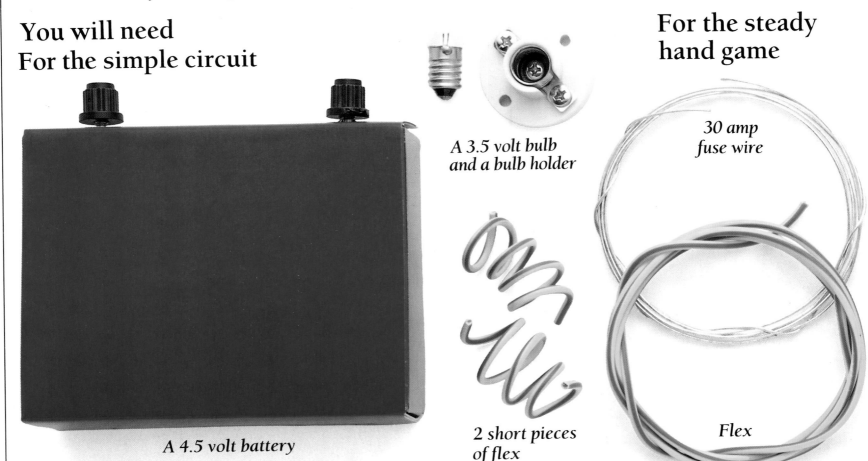

A 4.5 volt battery

A 3.5 volt bulb and a bulb holder

2 short pieces of flex

For the steady hand game

30 amp fuse wire

Flex

Making a simple circuit

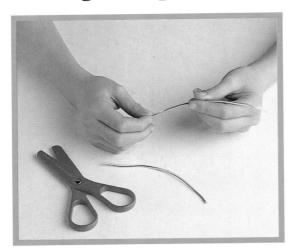

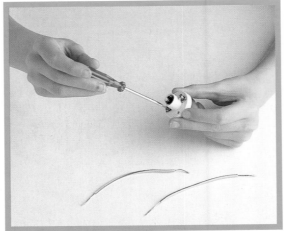

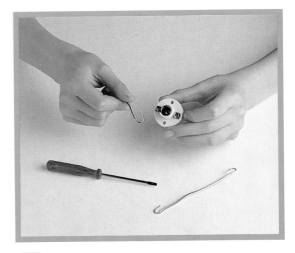

1 Cut about 2 cm of plastic from each end of the two pieces of flex. Twist the little wires together to make neat ends.

2 Undo the screws of the bulb holder slightly, by slotting the screwdriver into them and turning it anticlockwise.

3 Make a small hook at one end of each piece of flex. Then hook the two pieces of flex around the screws of the bulb holder.

42

Sticky tape

A cardboard box with a lid

A 3.5 volt bulb

A bulb holder

A 4.5 volt battery

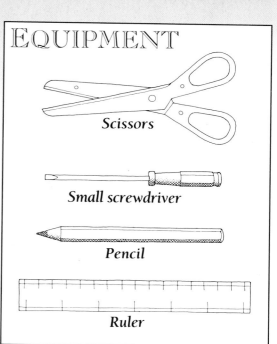

EQUIPMENT

Scissors

Small screwdriver

Pencil

Ruler

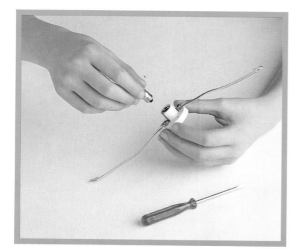

4 Do both screws up tightly, by slotting the screwdriver into them and turning it clockwise. Screw the bulb into the holder.

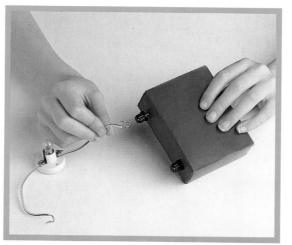

5 Undo the small knobs on top of the battery (the terminals). Hook the end of one piece of flex onto a terminal and do it up.

6 Hook the end of the other piece of flex onto the second terminal. The light will go on. To make it stay on, do up the terminal.

THE STEADY HAND GAME

What to do

1 Cut a piece of fuse wire 40 cm long and another 15 cm long. Make a loop at one end of the short wire. Bend the long wire as shown.

2 Thread the wavy wire through the loop. Make two holes in the box lid with a pencil. Push the ends of the wire through them.

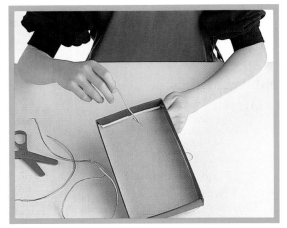

3 Cut two pieces of flex 20 cm long and another one 55 cm long. Strip the ends. Join one end of a 20 cm piece to the wavy wire.

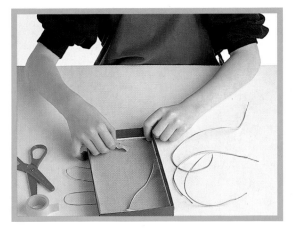

4 Tape the joined flex and wire to the inside of the box lid. Tape the other end of the wavy wire to the inside of the lid.

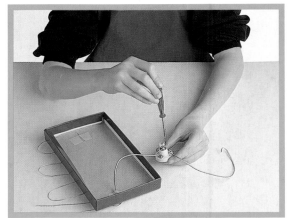

5 Screw the bulb into the bulb holder. Attach the two 20 cm pieces of flex to the bulb holder, as shown on page 42.

6 Make a small hole in the middle of the box lid*. Push the bulb up through it. Tape the bulb holder to the inside of the lid.

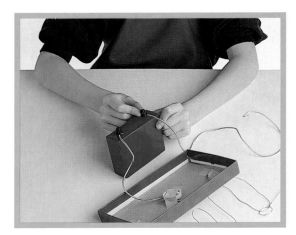

7 Join the free end of flex from the bulb holder to the battery. Attach one end of the long piece of flex to the other terminal.

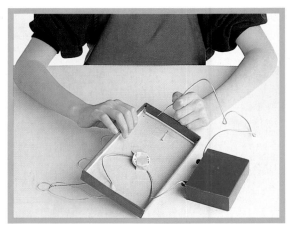

8 Make a small hole in one corner of the box lid with a pencil. Push the free end of the long flex up through it.

9 Put the battery in the box. Join the end of the wire loop to the end of the long piece of flex. Put the lid on the box.

Ask an adult to help you.

THE STEADY HAND GAME

Each person has to try and pass the loop all the way along the bendy wire without touching it and making the light go on.

The more bends you make in the wire, the harder the game is to play.

Once you have made the game, you can decorate the box with shapes cut out of aluminium foil.

SIMPLE CIRCUIT

The light goes on when everything is joined together to make a circuit (a complete circle for electricity to go around). Electricity runs from the battery to the bulb, then back to the battery. If you unhook a flex from the battery, the circuit is broken and the light goes out.

45

SCIENTIST'S KIT

You do not need special equipment like test tubes to do your science experiments. You can find most of the things you need at home. Start collecting useful equipment and keep it in a special box or cupboard. Here are some of the most useful things to have in your kit.

Glue stick

Food colouring or ink, for water experiments

Sticky tape

Jars of all sizes, for doing experiments with liquids

String

Torch, for experiments with light

4.5 volt batteries. You can buy these in hardware shops and model shops.

A funnel, for water experiments

A small magnifying glass

Horseshoe magnets. You can buy these in hardware shops.

3.5 volt bulbs, which you also buy in hardware shops.

Bulb holders for the bulbs shown above

Flex and fuse wire, available from hardware shops

A prism, for experiments with light. You can buy one from school suppliers.

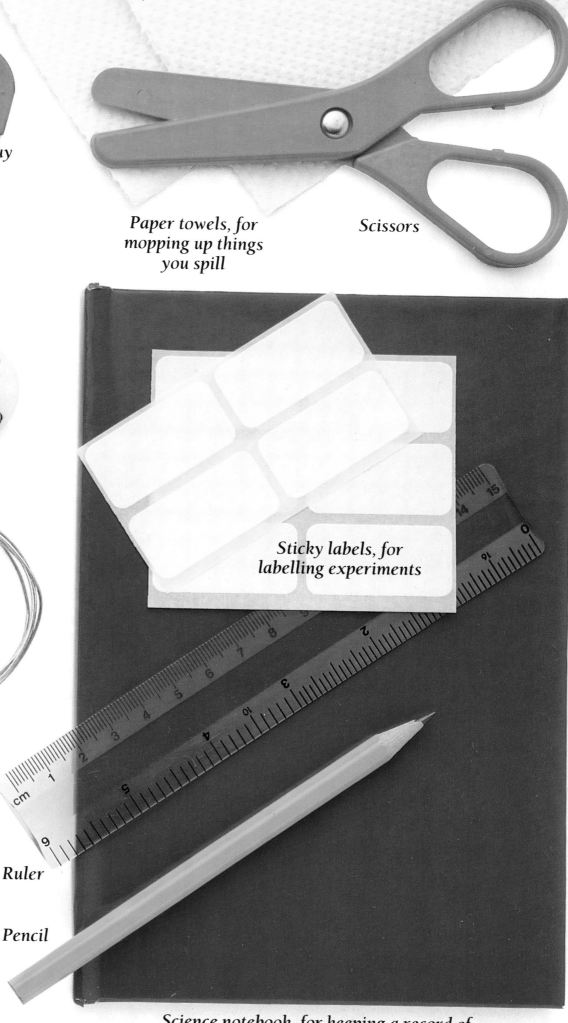

Paper towels, for mopping up things you spill

Scissors

Sticky labels, for labelling experiments

Ruler

Pencil

Science notebook, for keeping a record of all your experiments and their results

BENDING LIGHT

Light always shines in straight lines. If you shine a torch in a dark room, you see a straight beam. If you block part of the beam with an object, you see a shadow, because light cannot bend round things. Sometimes, though, light does seem to bend, as these two quick experiments show.

You will need

A prism

A glass of water

Some drinking straws

What to do

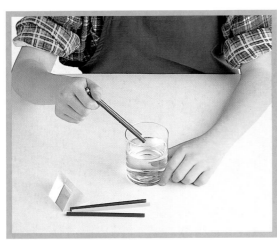

Stand some straws in the glass of water and look at them from the side. Then put some straws on a table and lay the prism on top.

Why does it happen?

Light travels fastest through air. When it enters water or glass, it slows down and changes direction a little, making things look as if they bend.

Bent straws

The straws beneath the prism look as if they are bent in two places and the straws in the glass of water appear to bend as they enter the water.